Mary Anne Fitz-Gerald

Australian Furs and Feathers

Mary Anne Fitz-Gerald

Australian Furs and Feathers

ISBN/EAN: 9783337311575

Printed in Europe, USA, Canada, Australia, Japan

Cover: Foto ©Andreas Hilbeck / pixelio.de

More available books at **www.hansebooks.com**

AUSTRALIAN
FURS AND FEATHERS,

BY

MARY ANNE FITZ-GERALD.

Illustrated by W. T. Anderson.

SYDNEY AND BRISBANE.
EDWARDS, DUNLOP AND CO., LIMITED.

1889.

DEDICATION.

To The Hon. Lady Carrington, in appreciation of the deep interest she has manifested in all that concerns Australian Children, this book is, with kind permission, most respectfully dedicated by her Ladyship's humble and obedient servant,

The Authoress.

Sydney, September, 1889.

Preface.

IN this little book my endeavour has been to describe as briefly, and in as simple a manner as possible, some of the most remarkable of the Australian Animals.

I have not considered it necessary to use any scientific terms or classification in my descriptions; my chief object being to enlist the interest of my little countrymen and countrywomen in the natural history of the beautiful birds and other animals of their own "Sunny Land."

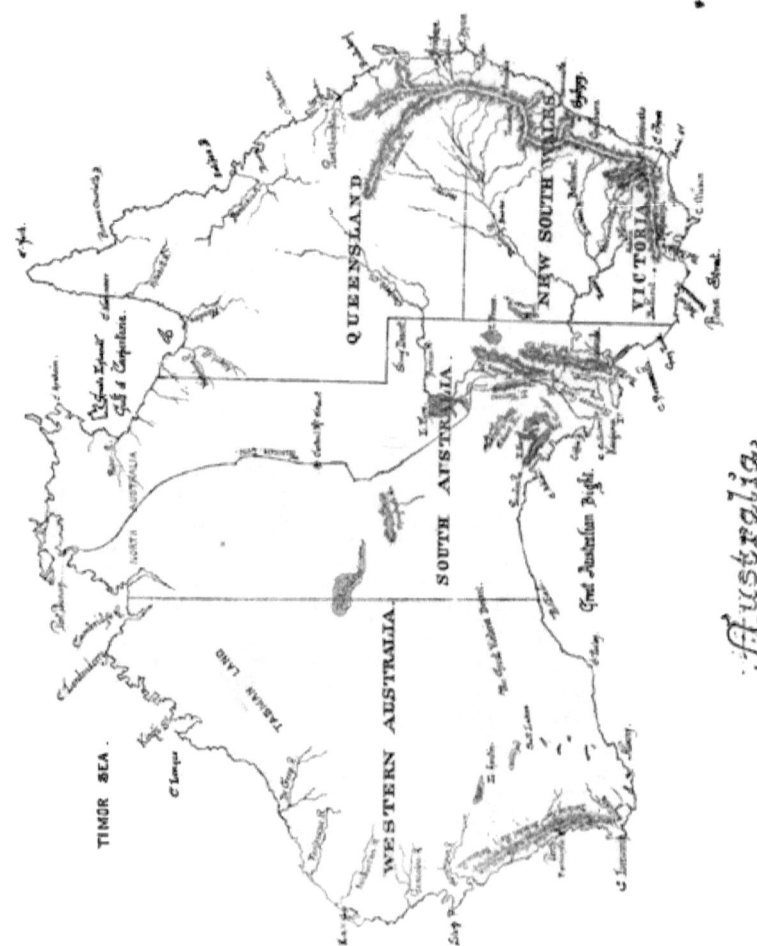

Australia.

AUSTRALIA, as the name indicates, is situated in the southern part of the world. It is just about one hundred years ago since Captain James Cook landed on the Eastern Coast and took possession of the island on behalf of his majesty King George III. of England. It is now divided into five colonies, each of which is ruled by a governor, appointed by Her Majesty Queen Victoria.

Australia is rich in mineral wealth, such as gold, silver, copper, tin, iron, and other metals, sides coal which is largely worked. In the forests are found many valuable timber trees, as the various kinds of Eucalypti, the Turpentine tree, Forest Oak, Cedar, Casuarina, Fragrant Rosewood, Beech, Banksias, Australian Pine, and others, all of which are extensively used either for building or other purposes. The harbour of Port Jackson is one of the finest in the world. At its entrance is the bold rocky promontory of North Head; on South Head now stands a lighthouse, from which the revolving electric light is seen for several miles around. Many cosey nooks and charming bays are to be seen along the shores of this beautiful harbour, and many lovely islets are scattered over its placid waters. It was upon its banks that the first settlement was formed, from which have sprung up the great capital cities of Sydney, Melbourne, Adelaide, Brisbane & Perth.

The Australian Blackman.
Aboriginal Kori.

The Blackman.

THE Blackman is a native of Australia. At one time thousands of these savages roamed over this Southern Land and were then its only possessors. They lived in camps made of the bark and branches of trees, which they called "Gunyahs" or "Wurleys," and hunted in the forests with boomerang and spear, for the different animals which served them for food. They fished in the streams and rivers, over which they paddled in their frail bark canoes called "Bokko yakko." In the bright moonlight they danced the Corrobboree, and sang their wild songs of joy and freedom.

Their bodies were painted with pipeclay and "karko" (red ochre), and they decorated their heads with the gay feathers of the "Wattee bah," (Lory Parrot) and other birds. The Cooee was a peculiar call used among the different tribes sometimes as a war-cry, at other times as a warning, or as an invitation to strangers. But since the white people came here about one hundred years ago, the aborigines have been gradually dying out, and soon will be remembered only by the names they have given to places and animals. In this book, the aboriginal names are printed in italics.

The Cockatoo.

The Cockatoo. *(Cacatua Galerita).*

COCKATOOS are very graceful looking birds with snow-white feathers and yellow crests. A flock of these beautiful white birds as they fly through the green forests looks extremely pretty, but their loud voices have a harsh disagreeable sound. They do not trouble themselves to build nests, but lay their eggs in the hollow limbs of trees, and there they hatch and rear their little ones. Their food consists of seeds of various kinds growing in the bush. They are very destructive to the farmers' crops of maize and wheat, and in the ripening seasons are seen in flocks of thousands about the neighbourhood of the fields. They seem to know they will come to harm if they are found trespassing, for one of their number will perch in a high tree close by, and, if he sees anyone approaching, will cry loudly to the feeding flock that will instantly rise and fly away screaming as if they were hurt. As pets, the *Curraways* readily learn to repeat words, most children have heard "Pretty Cocky." We should be very kind to the poor birds that are kept as pets, for we must remember that we have taken them away from their friends and home, and birds like the Cockatoos that live in flocks of hundreds in the forests, must no doubt sometimes long to be again with their companions in happy freedom.

The Swan.

The Swan. *(Cygnus Astratus)*.

WE are very proud of our beautiful Black Swan, not only because it belongs to our country alone, and is so tame gentle and harmless, but also because it is such a grand stately looking bird. It lives near lakes, ponds, lagoons and rivers, and swims on the water where it finds its food. Its nest is made of reeds and grass, on the margin of inland waters, and there it lays its eggs and hatches its young ones. So much is our queenly Swan admired that it has been taken over the sea to other lands, and while the little black children are watching its graceful movements on some lonely lake or stream in the Australian bush, the children of royalty may be praising its strange and rare beauty in their distant English home. Every year hundreds of these fine birds are killed to obtain the soft white down with which their breasts are covered. Some of the aboriginal names for the Swan are *Mullwee, Mulgo, Goljak Gullwanyick, &c.*

The Tallegalla.

The Talegalla. *(Talegalla).*

THE Talegalla or Brush Turkey is about the size of our domestic Turkey. These birds live in small families in the brushes along the coast and near the mountains. Their food consists of insects, berries, and seeds. Their flesh is considered very good, and the eggs are eaten by people living in the bush. They do not use their wings much, but when chased, fly into the lowest branches of a tree, and sit there very quietly, thus making easy game for the sportsman. The most remarkable feature in the habits of these birds is, that they do not sit upon their eggs like other birds, and hatch them in the usual way; but act in this matter somewhat like turtles do. About the beginning of Spring several of the birds unite, and form a mound or heap, by grasping in their feet the dead leaves, grass, etc., for some distance round and then throwing them backwards to one spot, till they complete the mound. Then the female bird lays her eggs at a depth of nearly three feet in this strange nest, and there they are left covered up until they are hatched by the heat of the decaying vegetable mass. The Native Pheasant, which inhabits the plains of Australia, builds a mound of sand mixed with leaves, grass, etc., in which its eggs are hatched like those of the Brush Turkey.

The Cuckoo. *(Chrysococcyx Lucidus).*

THERE are several kinds of Cuckoos found in Australia, they inhabit nearly every part of our country. The aborigines give them various names as *Ungkeewee, Dulaar, Judoorum,* &c. The little Bronze Cuckoo, shown in our plate, feeds on insects and caterpillars, which it finds among the branches and leaves of trees. Its movements are full of grace and activity. Like the Cuckoos of other countries it does not build a nest for itself, but lays its eggs in the nest of some other bird, sometimes it chooses the nest of the pretty "Blue Wren," or that of the sweet singing *Jeeda,* and leaves to these birds the task of hatching and rearing its young ones. Consequently with them the Cuckoo is no favorite. It seems strange that the Cuckoo should not build a nest and hatch her young ones like other birds do; but she wanders about very much, and most likely does not stay long enough in one place to sit upon her eggs, and so she distributes them among other birds. The Cuckoo's note has a mournful plaintive sound.

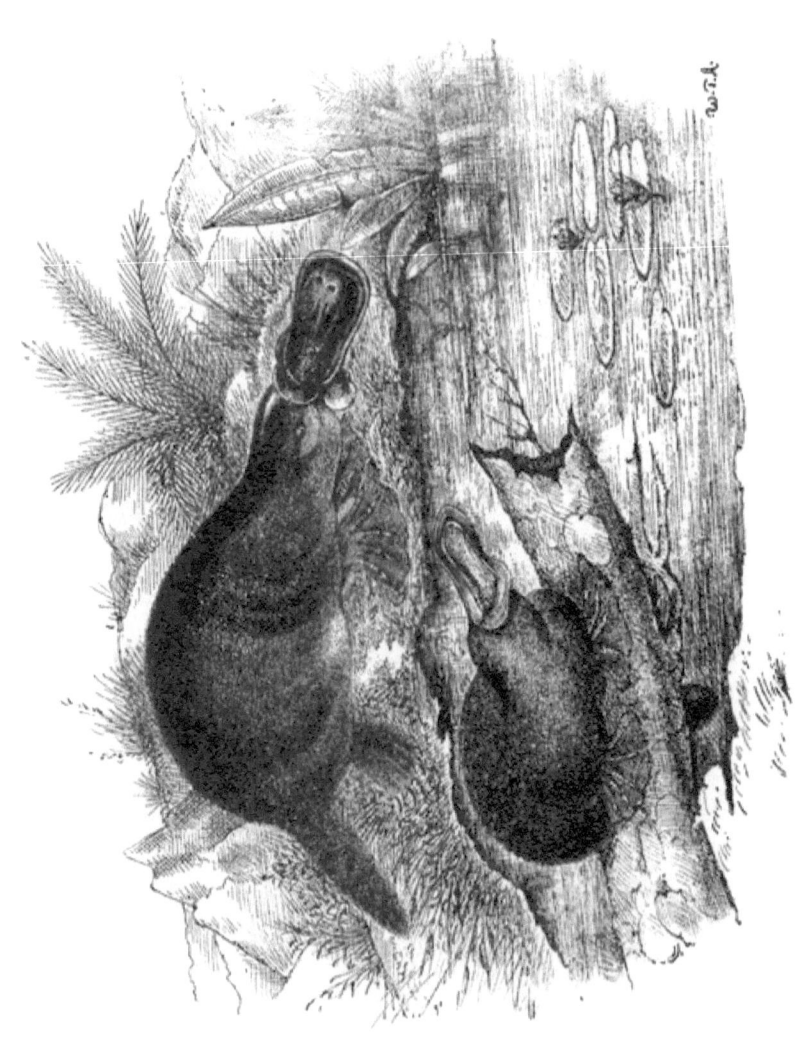

The Platypus. (*Ornithorhynchus Paradoxus*).

THE Platypus called also the Water Mole, and Duck Bill, spends most of its time in the water, where it finds its food by searching in the mud with its bill, just like the common duck does. It burrows in the banks of creeks, ponds, or lagoons. The entrance being made below the level of the water, the burrow is directed upwards and a second opening is formed in the bank above. If disturbed in the water, the Platypus will instantly dive beneath the surface, and enter its burrow. Like the Spiny Anteater, it lays eggs, from which it hatches its young. Its body is covered by a soft silky fur, but as these animals are rather scarce, and not easily caught, the fur is not in general use. The flesh is eaten by the blacks, who say, "*Mullangong* is *budgeree patta.*"

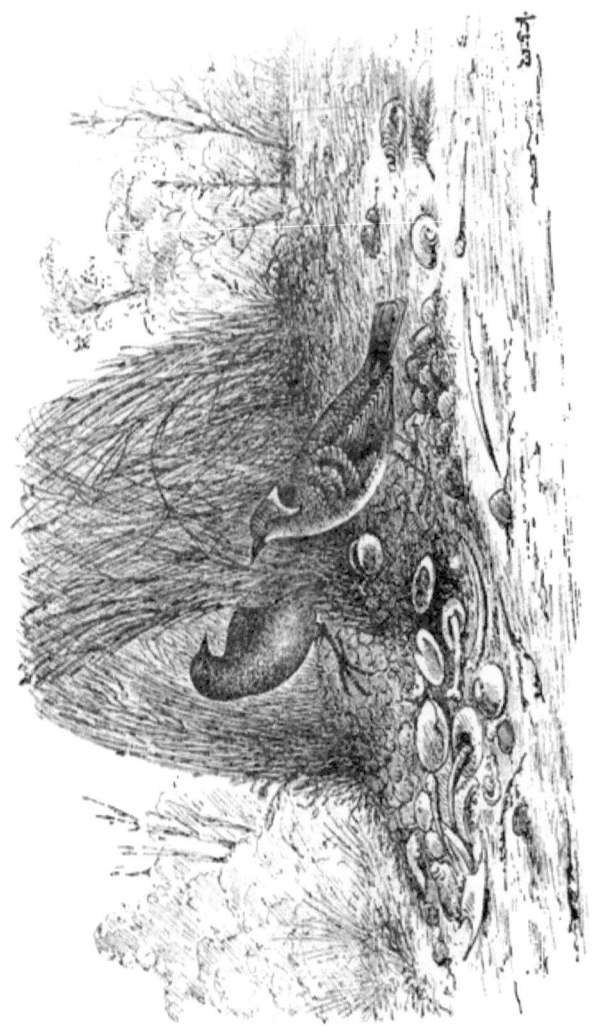
The Spotted Bower Bird.

The Spotted Bower Bird.
(Chlamydodera Maculata).

THE Bower Birds, like most of the Australian animals have different Native names as *Cowry, Qulara, Tewinga,* &c. They inhabit scrubs and brushes generally, but more particularly those between the Coast and Dividing Range, on the eastern side. They feed on figs, berries and other wild fruits, which grow very abundantly in these localities. There are about six different kinds of these birds in Australia, all having the same peculiar and remarkable habit of constructing bowers, open at both ends, which they use at certain times for playing places, where they chase each other in and out, just like laughing boys and girls do in their merry happy play. But you will say, "how can *birds* build a bower?" I will tell you. Several of the birds unite in forming a foundation, by weaving sticks and twigs together on the ground, and from the edges of this platform they raise the side walls of the bower by interweaving small twigs and tall grasses. These walls converge till they nearly meet at the top: they are gaily decorated with the brightest and most beautiful feathers. All around the entrances the birds strew every pretty object they can find in the bush, as bleached bones, coloured pebbles, snail shells, &c., some of which they bring from long distances. They build their nests in the low branches of trees.

Robins.

The Robin. *(Petroica Goodenovii).*

THERE are several kinds of Robins in our country, each kind receiving a distinguishing name from the aborigines. Thus the Scarlet Breasted Robin is called *Gooba*, the Red Capped Robin, *Menegedang*, and *Mulway*, the Hooded Robin, *Jilbut*, the Scrub Robin, *Trokaroo*, the Grey Breasted Robin, *Bamboora*, &c. Some of them inhabit the dense brushes near the coast, while others are seen only in open plains where there are not many trees. They generally live in pairs, together, and seek the most secluded parts of the plain or brush, passing the whole day singing their cheerful happy songs, and feeding on tiny insects. They build a very compact nest in the lower branches of trees, where the female bird lays three small eggs. Our little Robins resemble very much in their habits the European Robins, for they are very friendly and will hop about the dwellings of the people who live in the bush. In the Spring time they flock about the gardens and orchards of the farmers, without the least fear.

The Magpie.

The Magpie. *(Gymnorhina Tibicen).*

THE Magpie, known also as the piping Crow, is one of our sweetest warblers. It is called *Goorebat*, and *Koorakoola* by some of the aborigines and *Curluck* by others. They are cheerful birds, and are always heard singing their sweet songs in the early morning, as they flit about among the green trees, in flocks of twenty or thirty. They build a large untidy looking nest in the tree tops, which is often discovered by the eager screams of the parent bird, to keep away intruders. The *Goorebats* are very friendly and easily tamed, and if the least protection is offered to them by the settlers they become so familiar that they will approach their dwellings, in small flocks and perch on the surrounding fences. They feed entirely on insects, such as locusts and grasshoppers, they also eat centipedes and worms. When tamed the Magpie will learn to whistle and repeat words, and imitate the voices of different animals. Sometimes it seems a saucy bird, especially when it pretends to cry like the dear baby that we all love, but we know that the Magpie does not mean to annoy us, but only to amuse itself. We must not be angry either if the Magpie hops off with a spoon, or any other small article, in its bill, because it is a very active playful bird, and will repay us for all its little tricks by singing a cheerful happy song.

The Dollar Bird.

The Dollar Bird (*Eurystomus Australis*).

THE Australian Roller is commonly known as the Dollar Bird. It receives this name because of a spot of silvery white feathers in the centre of each wing, which resembles in shape the coin called a dollar. The aboriginal name is *Natykin*. It is a bold and daring bird, and not easily frightened. It nests in hollow limbs of trees, and in the hatching season the male bird always keeps close to where his mate is sitting, and guards the nest very carefully. Its food consists of insects which it catches in the air, and among the branches of trees. It seems to like dull gloomy weather best, for then it is most active and noisy, and its curious chattering song is constantly heard as it flies about the tree tops, generally with its mate. During the middle of the day the Dollar Bird remains sitting quietly on a tree, and does not seem inclined to move till evening comes on.

Opossums.

The Opossum. *(Vulpine phalangista, Viverrine phalangista).*

THERE are many different kinds of Opossums in Australia, such as the Ring Tailed Opossums Common Opossums, &c. Some of the aboriginal names for them are, *Pildra, Namee, Mallooreta, &c.* They sleep all day in the hollow limbs of trees, and then seem to be drowsy lazy creatures, but how different they look in the bright moonlight nimbly running about among the branches of the stately gum tree, seeking for the freshest and greenest leaves, and *Kong golias* (gum blossoms)! They are very seldom seen on the ground excepting when removing from one tree to another. Opossums are quiet harmless animals, and are very pretty and graceful in appearance. Their coats are thick and woolly, and for these furry coverings many thousands are killed every year. In our own country the skins are much used for rugs, muffs and tippets and they are also largely exported to other countries. The flesh is eaten by people living in the bush. The Aborigines when cooking the Opossum place it in a blazing fire without the least preparation, when the fur is well singed and the skin burnt, it is considered to be cooked and fit for eating, and is a welcome meal for the blackman his lubra, pickaninnies and *dingoes*.

The Jabiru.

The Jabiru. (*Mycteria Australis*.)

THE Australian "Jabiru" very much resembles the birds belonging to the same family inhabiting South America and Western Africa. "Jabiru" is the name given by the natives of Brazil. The aboriginal name for the Jabiru is *Burrienna*. It is always found near, water sometimes on the banks of salt-water creeks, but more frequently in lagoons and swamps where it wades about seeking for frogs, fish, and other animals found in marshy places. It is often seen on headlands near the sea, preferring the most open and exposed situations where it can see all around, and is thus enabled to escape from danger. It flies very slowly, with its wings extended to their full length, which is about seven feet. The flesh of the Jabiru has a fishy taste, caused by the food upon which it feeds. In its native state it is very shy and timid, and very wary, but when domesticated, as it has been sometimes, it is a most friendly and social bird.

The Kangaroo.

The Kangaroo. *(Macropus Major)*.

THE Great Kangaroo is the largest of the Australian animals. It is extremely graceful in appearance especially when seen bounding through the forest. It then uses only its hind legs, and balances itself with its long powerful tail. The female Kangaroo, called *Woowee*, like the Wallaby, Opossum, Bandicoot, &c., carries her young ones in a pouch until they are old enough to take care of themselves. Kangaroos feed upon grass, and are constantly hunted and killed, for they crowd upon the cattle and sheep runs in immense numbers, and would soon eat up the pasture. They are also hunted for sport by horsemen, who use dogs trained for the purpose, and a "Kangaroo hunt" is considered very good sport. Often when chased very closely, the "Old Man" Kangaroo, or "Boomer" as it is also called, will stand upright against a tree, and if a dog should approach too near, with one blow of its powerful hind leg will lay it dead. The aborigines hunted and killed the Kangaroos with their sharp pointed spears. Another mode too of killing them was by surrounding a large number in the forest, and closing them in gradually, when the men and women would rush upon them with their *nulla nullas, waddies* and other weapons. Kangaroo skins are largely exported to other countries, and when tanned they make the best of leather.

The Lyre Bird.

The Lyre Bird. *(Menura Superba).*

THE Lyre Bird derives its name from the peculiar shape of the male bird's tail, which resembles in form a stringed musical instrument called the "Lyre," which was much used in former times in other countries. The blacks call the Lyre Bird *Beleck Beleck*, and *Boolangara*. It lives in the brushes along the coast, and near the coast range of mountains generally; and feeds upon various insects which it finds by scraping the ground with its feet like our domestic fowls do. It rarely flies into trees, but builds a large deep nest on ledges of rock, old stumps and fallen trees—

always near the ground. The Lyre Bird is very shy; when pursued it runs through the undergrowth of timber with great speed, and gives the sportsman much trouble. Its natural call is loud and rather pleasing. But it has wonderful power as a mocking bird, and can change its voice in an instant from the "Cat Bird's" curious wailing song, to the *Kukuburra's* loud laugh, and then to the *Dingo's* dreary howl, and again to the low soft note of the *Wonga* pigeon. It will also imitate such sounds as the sharpening of a saw, or the cracking of a stockman's whip, and so this clever mimic seems to amuse itself in the solitary brushes. These beautiful birds are far scarcer now than formerly, as they are much sought after for the tail feathers, which are sold in large numbers.

The Goburra. *(Dacelo Gigas.)*

THE Goburra is also called the Laughing Jackass, and Settler's Clock, the latter name because its loud strange laugh is heard at early morning and again at sun-set. The Aborigines of the various districts have different names for it, as *Kukuburra, Goburra,* and *Gogoburra,* all given in imitation of its curious note. It is also known as the "Giant Kingfisher," and "Great Brown Kingfisher," because it belongs to a tribe of birds called Kingfishers, but the Goburra does not live near water nor seek for fish. It frequents different localities, the rich brushes along the coast, also the forests and brushes near the mountain ranges. Although so fond of uttering its wild laugh, the Goburra is a grave serious looking bird, and no doubt its laughing is not always indicative of mirth, but is the natural sound of its voice. Like the Cockatoo, the Goburra lays its eggs, which are white and almost round, in the hollow limbs of trees. The male bird is very watchful in the hatching season. It is most valuable as a destroyer of vermin, and particularly for killing small snakes and lizards. It also eats grubs and worms. So useful is this bird considered, that a law has been made to protect it from wilful injury.

The Australian Hedgehog.
(Echidna Hystrix.)

THE Echidna, more generally known as the Spiny Anteater, and Australian Hedgehog is called *Janocumbine Nyoongarn*, &c. by the black people who eat its flesh and say it is *Budgeree Patta* (good food). The whole of its body is covered with black or brown hair, and the upper portion has a covering of spines or quills as well. The Echidna can extend its tongue which is very long, beyond its beak or snout, it is covered with a sticky substance to which ants and other insects adhere; and in this strange manner the Anteater catches its prey.

There are no teeth in its jaws, but in their place are horny ridges that serve instead. It is a quiet timid creature, but when teazed or disturbed will roll itself into the shape of a ball, and then the spines only can be seen, and as they are very sharp and strong they serve to shield it from harm. Its long sharp claws are well fitted for burrowing, which it does with wonderful rapidity, especially if the soil is loose or porous.

The Ibis.

The Ibis. *(Geronticus Spinicollis.)*

THE Straw necked Ibis, so named from the straw coloured feathers growing upon its neck has been found only in Australia. The black people call it *Yambull-bell* and *Muloora*. It inhabits places where lagoons are numerous, for in them it finds the food it likes best; such as shell-fish, frogs, and water insects generally. It also eats grasshoppers. The Ibis is rather a shy bird, and not easily approached. When walking over the ground it looks very stately and graceful. They often perch on low trees, and fly in large numbers like ducks and geese. A similar bird to the

White Ibis of our country is found in the warm parts of Asia and also in Africa, where it was once held sacred, and was worshipped by the people of Egypt, and when dead its body was preserved by being embalmed. Besides the Straw necked Ibis and the White Ibis, there is another beautiful bird belonging to the same family in our country called the "Glossy Ibis."

The Dingo.

The Dingo. *(Canis Dingo).*

THE Dingoes, or Native dogs of Australia, were at one time very numerous, but their numbers are lessening every year. Being deprived of their natural prey the Kangaroo, Wallaby, Bandicoot, etc., the Dingoes have become very troublesome in the settled districts, killing the cattle and sheep, and worrying others so severely that many die from exhaustion caused by loss of blood. In consequence of these bad practices, dingoes are constantly poisoned, trapped, and shot, in their native wilds. Often whole families of dingo puppies are destroyed by stockmen when they are found in hollow logs or crevices of rocks. The Dingo is not so faithful nor so useful as our domestic dog, as it is difficult to be tamed, and will obey but one master. It is generally supposed that the blacks made use of the *Warragals* for hunting the animals which served as a feast for the dog and his dusky masters.

The Emu.

The Emu. *(Dromiceus Australis).*

THE Emu is a grand stately looking bird, and except the Ostrich which lives in Africa is the largest bird in the world, being from five to six feet in height. At a distance its feathers look very much like coarse hair. Some of the native names for the Emu are *Moregnonder*, *Wooroocathie* and *Bunggeera*. When speared, the Emu afforded a splendid feast for the black hunter, who we are told used to make an oven in the clay, in which the bird was cooked, without even being plucked. For some reason unknown to us, its flesh was not allowed to be eaten by the young men or boys. The Emu is now seen chiefly in the interior although at one time it inhabited most parts of Australia. It feeds on herbs and seeds of grasses, and builds no nest, but simply scrapes a shallow hole in the ground, and there lays its eggs, and hatches its young ones. The eggs which are large and beautiful are often set by jewellers in gold and silver, and made into ornaments, such as inkstands, cups and caskets; all very pretty and much admired. Emu Oil is largely used by bushmen as a remedy for aches and pains. The flesh of the young bird is considered very good. I am sorry to say our noble bird is every year becoming scarcer, as it is often hunted and killed for mere sport, while thousands of its eggs are destroyed.

The Finch.

The Finch. *(Amadina Guttata).*

THERE are about twenty different kinds of Finches in Australia, each kind differing somewhat from the other in appearance and habits. The Aborigines call them by various names such as *Weebong, Jeeree, Goolungagga, Ingadamoon,* &c. They mostly inhabit grassy patches in the forests, or stony ridges, or flats where small trees grow. They do not fly in large flocks like parrots and cockatoos, but keep together in small families, and rarely fly into very high trees. None of them sing as sweetly as the finches of other lands. Their voices have rather a sad mournful sound;

but if our little Finches were better known, and if as much trouble were taken to teach them as is bestowed on the training of the Bullfinches in other countries, I think it is very likely they would reward us with many a sweet song. They are very pretty lively little creatures and are easily tamed.

The Vampire Bat,
Or Flying Fox.

The Vampire Bat. *(Pteropus funereus).*

THE Vampire Bat called *Lagker* and *Teewalla* by the blacks, is known also as the Great Fruit Bat, and Flying Fox, the latter name on account of the shape of its head, which bears some resemblance to the head of the fox. These large bats live in the brushes, where they sleep all day in immense numbers, suspended by their feet from the strong limbs of trees. At one time their only food was figs and wild berries, but since the settlers have cultivated orchards, they have become very troublesome, and will fly long distances to reach an orchard, especially when peaches are in season, and will eat and destroy large quantities of fruit. They are therefore shot by the settlers, and their homes in the brushes are often attacked, when thousands of them are killed while they are soundly sleeping. There are several different kinds of bats in Australia, but the Flying Fox is by far the largest of them. Its body is covered by a fine silky hair, its wings are strong and leathery. It obtains the name of Vampire from its resemblance to that kind of bat inhabiting South America, and the southern parts of Asia. The true Vampires are said to suck the blood of other animals, and many dismal stories are told of their attacks, even upon human beings when asleep.

The Crested Oropica.

The Crested Oreoica. *(Oreoica gutturalis).*

THE Oreoica more commonly called the Bell Bird, is found everywhere in the Southern portions of Australia, but not very plentifully in any particular locality. It is generally seen in small companies in the open parts of the forests hopping about in a sprightly manner. Its food consists of seeds of various sorts, besides insects, grubs, and caterpillars. What is most remarkable concerning this bird is, that it can use its voice in such a way that it appears to sound as if it were uttered at some distance from where the bird is sitting. This peculiar power is possessed by some human beings, such persons being termed Ventriloquists. It is a power that can be cultivated, but very often, as with the Bell Bird, it is quite natural, and may be unknown to its possessor. The Bell Bird has two kinds of songs, each ending with a note that sounds like the ringing of a bell. The Aboriginal names are *Bokurba, Yumbeena, Telwalla &c.* There is a pretty bird in New South Wales called the Bell Bird, whose song resembles the sound of distant sheep bells. It dwells only in damp marshy places.

The Warbling Grass Parrakeet,

The Warbling Grass Parrakeet or Zebra Parrot. (Melopsittacus undulatus).

THESE beautiful ground Parrakeets are seen in the early morning, and at dusk in the evening, seeking among the grass for the various seeds which serve them for food. They seem to be very fond of each other, for they always fly together in flocks of many hundreds, and warble their cheerful songs all through the day. They are extremely gay in appearance, and no prettier sight can be seen in our forests than a flock of these brilliant creatures. They nest like most others of their tribe, in the hollow limbs and trunks of trees. Although they seem so full of joy and gladness when in large numbers together, yet they appear to be just as happy and contented when they are kept in single pairs in a cage. The Zebra Parrots have been taken to England, where they thrive well and are universally admired. The term "Zebra" has been applied to them on account of the Zebra-like markings on their feathers. The Aboriginal names are *Budgeree-gar* and *Betcherrygah,* both referring to the beauty of their appearance.

The Wombat.

The Wombat. *(Phascolmys Wombat).*

THE Wombat burrows a hole in the ground, where it sleeps all through the day, and seems to be very comfortable in this gloomy dwelling. At night, when all around is quiet and still, it wakes up and leaves its burrow to seek for roots, which it grinds with its strong sharp teeth. It also eats fresh green grass. It is a dull stupid-looking creature, but is timid and perfectly harmless. When attacked or teased, it utters a hissing sound. The flesh of the Wombat is very delicate and tender, and often formed a savoury meal for the hungry Aborigines, and was cooked in the same simple manner as the Opossum and other small animals. Its fur is coarse and strong. These animals are particularly numerous in the southern parts of Australia, where "Wombat holes" often cause a dangerous fall to the horseman as he rides through the bush at full speed, perhaps after a mob of wild cattle.

The Xerophila.

The Xerophila. *(Xerophila leucopsis).*

THIS little bird is found in many parts of Australia, but not in any other country. *Yinko, Kirraway,* and *Midgee* are some of the names given to it by the Aborigines. It feeds on seeds of grasses, and other small plants, and is generally seen on the ground, where it hops about very quickly, and appears to be a busy, active little creature. It sometimes flies into low trees, and from one tree to another, in small flocks of about a dozen or sixteen. Its nest is made of dried grass, moss, spiders' webs, and dead leaves, all joined together; and often built among the scented blossom of the wattle tree. The Xerophila is a very familiar sprightly little creature, and easily tamed; but is not a singing bird, and is chiefly remarkable for belonging to a genus or class confined to our country alone.

ERRATA.

Australia.

Twelfth line, read; *besides*.

Magpie.

Second page, fourth line, read; *feed chiefly*.

www.ingramcontent.com/pod-product-compliance
Lightning Source LLC
Chambersburg PA
CBHW020144170426
43199CB00010B/873